TINY TIM
THE
LAST GIFT

Tiny Tim: The Last Gift

Copyright © 2025 by Gary J. Rose. All rights reserved.

The content contained within this book may not be reproduced, duplicated or transmitted without direct written permission from the author or the publisher. Under no circumstances will any blame or legal responsibility be held against the publisher, or author, for any damages, reparation, or monetary loss due to the information contained within this book, either directly or indirectly. Legal Notice: This book is copyright protected. It is only for personal use. You cannot amend, distribute, sell, use, quote or paraphrase any part, or the content within this book, without the consent of the author or publisher. Disclaimer Notice: Please note the information contained within this document is for educational and entertainment purposes only. All effort has been executed to present accurate, up to date, reliable, complete information. No warranties of any kind are declared or implied. Readers acknowledge that the author is not engaged in the rendering of legal, financial, medical or professional advice. The content within this book has been derived from various sources. Please consult a licensed professional before attempting any techniques outlined in this book. By reading this document, the reader agrees that under no circumstances is the author responsible for any losses, direct or indirect, that are incurred as a result of the use of the information contained within this document, including, but not limited to, errors, omissions, or inaccuracies.

ISBN: 979-89985106-8-7 (hardback)
        979-8-9985106-9-4 (paperback)

Printed in the United States of America

Tiny Tim
THE LAST GIFT

A Christmas Novella

GARY J. ROSE

Foreword

From the Author

There are few works of literature that have endured with such lasting emotional power and moral clarity as A Christmas Carol by Charles Dickens. First published in 1843, it has transcended time, language, and medium — not only as a story of ghosts and redemption, but as a living embodiment of the spirit of compassion and the enduring possibility of change.

It is a tale that has inspired millions — whether through the printed page, stage, radio, film, or television. Each generation has found something of itself in the figure of Ebenezer Scrooge, in the steadfast love of the Cratchit family, and most of all, in the fragile, hopeful heart of young Tiny Tim.

As a novelist and screenwriter, I have always been drawn to stories that speak to something eternal within us — the part that resists cynicism, yearns for grace, and believes in second chances. In 2023, I published a sequel titled Christmas Carol: The Next Chapter, which explored what might happen in the years after Scrooge's fateful Christmas Eve transformation. The response to that story was overwhelmingly warm — not just because it continued a beloved classic, but because it honored what Dickens gave us: a call to conscience wrapped in a tale of redemption.

And yet, one question remained.

What ever became of Tiny Tim?

It's a question I couldn't shake. Tim, after all, was the beating heart of Dickens' original tale — the symbol of all that was good, vulnerable, and worth saving. His survival was more than a plot point; it was a miracle born of Scrooge's transformation. But what happens when miracles fade? What becomes of a child whose life was once changed… when the world around him changes again?

That question led me here — to Tiny Tim: The Last Gift.

This story follows Tim as an adult. Life, as it tends to do, has offered both blessings and burdens. The warmth of Scrooge's reformation has dimmed. Loved ones have passed. The city Tim once viewed with wonder has become colder, more distant, more self-involved. Faith, for Tim, is no longer easy. It's a struggle — the same kind many of us face in our own lives.

And then comes Christmas.

This novel is not a retelling of Dickens. It is, I hope, a respectful echo — a spiritual sequel that honors the heart of the original while giving voice to a character whose story deserves to be told. There are no dancing sugarplums or hollow nostalgia here. There is loss. There is doubt. But there is also hope — and the reminder that the greatest gifts we give are not wrapped in ribbons, but offered through kindness, selflessness, and love.

It is my sincere hope that Tiny Tim: The Last Gift brings you warmth, reflection, and perhaps even a renewed sense of what it means to carry the spirit of Christmas not just for a day… but for a lifetime. Enjoy.

Chapter 1

Snow had begun to fall on the rooftops of London, soft and slow, like ash drifting down from a candle long since extinguished. It dusted the old iron railings that ringed the churchyard and settled on the black hats of mourners gathered in silence. Even the bells, though they tolled the hour, seemed to muffle themselves out of respect for the man they rang for.

Ebenezer Scrooge was dead.

The Reverend's voice rose from the stone pulpit, echoing beneath the high arches of St. Martin's, reciting verses about the final journey, the reward of grace, the promise of redemption. But for Timothy Cratchit—Tiny Tim, once upon a time—it was hard to concentrate on the words. His hands, clasped before him, had gone numb in the cold. Not from winter, but from the weight of grief.

He hadn't cried. Not yet. And that surprised him.

Scrooge was supposed to outlive them all, Tim thought. The man had survived bitterness, haunting, transformation, pneumonia twice, and the unrelenting scorn of early Victorian society. After his change, he seemed untouchable. Eternal. A force of relentless generosity in a world determined to forget the poor.

And yet now, he lay beneath the earth.

Tim stood near the front of the chapel, his cane resting against the pew. The seat beside him was empty—symbolically left open, some had said, in honor of Scrooge's solitude in life. But to Tim, it felt like something else. A void.

He remembered the first Christmas after Scrooge's transformation—how the old man had appeared at their door in his long coat and top hat, holding a goose in one arm and a ledger of donations in the other. How he had laughed, so awkwardly, so honestly. How he had insisted on learning their names—not as a benefactor, but as something more. Something close to family.

It was Scrooge who paid for Tim's surgeries. Scrooge who arranged for his first pair of crutches. Scrooge who had wept with joy when Tim took his first unaided steps across the parlor rug.

And now Scrooge lay beneath a blanket of earth, his stone bearing a simple inscription:

Ebenezer Scrooge – A Friend To All.

The Reverend offered a final prayer, and as the congregation began to shift, Tim felt a gentle hand on his shoulder. One of the church elders leaned in and whispered, "Would you say a few words?"

Tim nodded slowly and stepped forward to the pulpit, hands trembling slightly as he adjusted the collar of his overcoat. The church was packed, not just with dignitaries and business partners, but with the ordinary—the shopkeepers, paupers, and orphans whose lives had quietly been changed by a man once called miser.

He cleared his throat, eyes settling on Scrooge's simple stone marker below.

"When I was a child," he began, voice steady, "I thought Ebenezer Scrooge was the richest man in London. Not because of his bank accounts or his ledgers, but because he gave me a chance to live."

A few heads bowed. One woman quietly dabbed her eyes with a handkerchief.

"He once told me that it is never too late to become the person you were meant to be. That redemption is not earned through wealth or words, but through acts of kindness, quietly offered, often unseen.

"I saw a man transform—not because ghosts frightened him into it, but because he allowed his heart to be changed. And in doing so, he changed all of us.

"He became a friend. A second father. A reminder that joy is not a possession, but a gift we give to one another.

"He gave that joy freely, especially at Christmas. And though he is gone, the echo of his laughter and the warmth of his generosity will remain. In me. In you. In all who choose compassion over indifference.

"Today, we do not bury a miser. We lay to rest a man redeemed.

"And I will carry Christmas forward—for him. For us all."

The silence afterward was deeper than any prayer. The air itself seemed to pause.

Tim remained as the mourners left, nodding politely, accepting gloved hands and murmured condolences. He stood alone at the grave, cane in hand, breath misting as the snow thickened.

"I suppose it falls to me now," he whispered.

Behind him, a voice stirred. "Falls to you, what?"

Tim turned. It was Martha, his older sister, wrapped in a wool cloak, her eyes as tired as his own.

"To keep Christmas," he said. "To carry it forward."

Martha stepped beside him. "You always have, Tim. You're the only one who still believes in all of it."

He managed a smile, though it felt hollow. "I believed because of him. Because he proved it was never too late."

They stood together a while longer, the wind threading through the bare trees.

"I'm not sure it's enough anymore," Tim admitted. "London's changed. The people are colder now. Christmas feels more like habit than heart."

Martha placed a hand on his shoulder. "Then maybe it's your turn to change it again."

He nodded but said nothing. A horse's whinny echoed nearby, and the sound of a carriage shifting in the slush brought them back to the present.

"I'll walk," Tim said softly.

Martha squeezed his hand. "I'll see you tonight. There's dinner at mine."

He smiled faintly and watched her leave, her figure slowly swallowed by the snow.

Tim let out a breath he hadn't realized he'd been holding. The snow was heavier now, blurring the outlines of gravestones and coating the cobblestones in white. It was the kind of snowfall that swallowed sound, made everything feel like a dream half-remembered.

He took a slow walk through the churchyard, past names he'd known as a child and names he never had the chance to learn. The city, beyond the black wrought-iron fence, carried on. Carriages passed. Children laughed. But here, in this place of rest, time seemed to hold its breath.

That night, Tim returned to the house he kept alone, a modest flat above the school where he taught. He set his cane by the door, lit a fire, and stared for a long time at the empty chair by the hearth—Scrooge's chair, gifted to him in the will. The leather was worn, the wood smooth from use. It smelled faintly of pipe smoke and peppermint.

The silence in the room was deep. Not heavy or suffocating—just... final.

On the mantle, a single envelope rested beside a sprig of holly. He hadn't noticed it before.

It was addressed in Scrooge's handwriting.

To Timothy Cratchit

For Christmas Eve. One Last Gift.

Tim's fingers hovered over the envelope, but he didn't open it. Not yet. Instead, he sat slowly in the chair and stared into the fire.

Outside, the snow fell harder. The windows frosted at the edges, curling with lace-like patterns. Somewhere in the distance, church bells rang again. The same ones from earlier, though fainter now, like a memory echoing across time.

He whispered into the fire, almost without realizing, "I'm not ready."

And for the first time in years, he wished that Scrooge would walk through the door, just once more, and tell him what to do next.

Chapter 2

THE CRATCHIT HOME HAD LONG since changed, but it still bore echoes of the past in every corner.

Martha's dining room was modest but warm, filled with the scent of cloves and rosemary and the faintest trace of wood smoke. It wasn't the same house they'd grown up in—not the threadbare flat off Camden Street with the drafty windows and squeaky stairs—but it might as well have been. The air held the same closeness. The laughter. The stories repeated so often they had taken on the quality of myth.

Belinda was already at the table, her hands busily folding napkins into ornate triangles no one would actually use. Peter sat at the far end, his glasses halfway down his nose, peering at the day's paper, though he rarely turned the page. It was just his way of being still.

Tim stood in the doorway a moment longer than he should have, unnoticed, taking in the scene. For a brief second, he could almost imagine himself ten again, peeking around the corner in hopes of sneaking an extra sweet.

But the illusion passed. He stepped forward, and Belinda looked up.

"You're late," she teased.

Tim shrugged, unwinding his scarf. "I walked."

"In this cold?" Peter glanced over his glasses. "You'll catch your death."

"I was already at a funeral," Tim said without thinking, and the room fell momentarily still.

Martha stepped in from the kitchen, apron dusted with flour. "Let's not start tonight in a graveyard," she said gently, offering a brief, maternal glance his way. "Tim's here now. That's what matters."

Tim forced a smile and pulled out a chair near the fire. The warmth felt good against his knees.

Belinda reached over and patted his hand. "We heard the service was beautiful."

"It was," he said, voice quiet. "It was everything he deserved."

No one asked him to elaborate. They didn't need to. They all knew how much Scrooge had come to mean to him—not just as a benefactor or employer, but something much harder to explain. Something closer to kin.

Peter cleared his throat, awkward in the silence. "The city paper ran a column. Called him 'The Ghost-Touched Philanthropist.' Said he changed half the charities in London before his death."

Martha smirked. "A little late for praise, isn't it? When he needed their cooperation, they wouldn't give him the time of day."

Tim nodded faintly. "They feared his past more than they trusted his change."

"People always remember the sin louder than the redemption," Peter murmured.

Martha returned to the table with a platter of roast and stewed carrots, setting it down between them with the practiced ease of a woman who had been holding this family together for decades. She moved without complaint, her motions second nature.

They ate slowly, the conversation shifting toward softer things—Peter's students, Belinda's new seamstress commission, the strange man on the tram who tried to sell them all "miracle hair oil." For a time, it almost felt like a normal evening. Almost.

But Tim found himself distracted. Every sound—the clink of a spoon, the creak of the chair—seemed louder than usual. The silence between laughs seemed longer. It was as though grief had dulled the edges of the world.

Midway through the meal, Martha poured him a second cup of tea and lingered behind his chair.

"He left you something, didn't he?" she asked softly.

Tim looked up. Her eyes weren't prying—just knowing.

"Yes," he admitted. "A letter. And the ledger."

Martha pulled out the chair beside him. "The same one?"

Tim nodded. "The very same. It's worn, but the pages are intact."

"Are you going to write in it?" she asked.

He hesitated. "I don't know. Part of me feels like I'd be trespassing. It was his."

"No," Martha said gently. "It was always yours, Tim. You were just waiting to hold the pen."

That struck him harder than he expected. He blinked and looked away.

The fire crackled in the hearth, throwing shadows across the table. Outside, the snow fell heavier now, sticking to windows and cobblestones. The world seemed muffled again, as though wrapped in wool.

Peter stood to fetch a bottle of cider from the sideboard. "Let's toast to him," he said. "To Scrooge."

"To Ebenezer," Belinda echoed, lifting her glass.

They all raised theirs—except Tim, who stared at the amber liquid for a long second before finally lifting it.

"To the man who taught us how to live by changing how he died," he said softly.

They clinked glasses.

And in that brief pause afterward, Tim felt something shift inside him. Not closure, exactly—but a kind of beginning.

As though the story wasn't over.

Just his chapter was about to start.

CHAPTER 3

THE CHALK SQUEAKED FAINTLY AS Tim scrawled the last equation on the board.

Outside, snow tapped softly against the tall windows of the schoolroom, like impatient fingers urging the lesson to end. The children fidgeted in their seats, jackets buttoned all the way up despite the glowing stove at the back of the room. Their cheeks were flushed from earlier play, but their attention was waning.

Tim laid the chalk down carefully and turned.

"And if a train leaves Liverpool at noon, traveling east at fifteen miles per hour," he said, smiling faintly, "how long will it take to arrive in York?"

Several hands shot up. Most were guesses. One boy offered "an hour," with all the confidence of a future prime minister.

Tim chuckled softly. "A fine guess, Thomas. But unfortunately, York is not next door to Liverpool."

There were groans, and a few heads thudded against desks in exaggerated despair.

"Alright," Tim said. "Let's stop torturing numbers and give them a rest. Dismissed."

Chairs scraped back. Books were shut with the urgency of freedom. Coats went flying over shoulders and boots clomped across the wooden floors like thunder.

One small girl—Elsie, red-haired and quiet—paused at the door, turned, and said, "Happy Christmas, Mr. Cratchit."

Tim's heart softened. "And to you, Miss Elsie. Stay warm."

When the room emptied, he remained at the front, staring at the chalkboard. The numbers blurred together. For a moment, he wasn't sure if he'd even written them correctly.

His thoughts kept drifting—back to the funeral, the weight of the envelope, the ledger.

He hadn't opened the letter yet. It sat on his writing desk at home, sealed and waiting. Something in him resisted. As though opening it would make Scrooge's death too real.

"You're miles away."

Tim turned.

Nathan stood in the doorway, bundled against the cold in a thick coat and scarf, his breath visible in the classroom's still air.

"You missed your appointment at the Foundation," Nathan said gently.

Tim exhaled and moved to the desk, collecting stray quills. "I know. I meant to come. I just... didn't."

Nathan stepped inside and closed the door. "You've always kept your promises. Especially to him."

"I never promised him I'd become him."

"No," Nathan said. "But he trusted you would."

Tim looked up, the lines around his eyes deeper today. "That's the problem. He believed in me more than I believe in myself."

Nathan crossed the room slowly. "Do you remember the first time you spoke to me?"

Tim blinked. "You mean when you were stealing from the bakery window?"

Nathan grinned. "It was a terrible plan. I was eleven and hungry. Thought a broken lock was fate."

"You were terrible at lying."

"You were terrible at catching."

They both chuckled, but the laughter faded quickly.

"You didn't turn me in," Nathan said, quieter now. "You handed me a roll and told me to come back the next day—to work it off."

"You did."

"I stayed."

Tim nodded. "Because Scrooge gave me the same choice once."

Nathan gestured toward the window. "Then keep giving it. Someone else is out there tonight, cold and hungry, hoping they'll be seen."

Tim stared outside. The snow had picked up again, blurring the iron gates around the schoolyard.

"I'm not him, Nathan."

"No," Nathan agreed. "You're you. That's the difference. And maybe the gift is supposed to change shape with every hand it passes through."

That line landed heavier than either of them expected.

Nathan straightened. "Come to the hall tonight. There's a new girl—barely speaks. She won't take food unless it's wrapped. But she keeps asking if someone named 'Cratchit' still lives here."

Tim frowned. "Did she give a name?"

"No. Just eyes like yours when you were her age."

Tim hesitated. "I'll think about it."

Nathan nodded once. "Don't think too long. It's Christmas in two days. And some gifts don't wait."

Then he left, the door swinging shut behind him.

Tim stood alone again in the quiet classroom. The chalkboard still bore the equation no one had solved. Behind it, the fire had gone low.

He looked at the board for a long moment, then erased it slowly, watching the numbers disappear under the sweep of the cloth.

CHAPTER 4

TIM SAT AT THE WRITING desk in his flat, staring at the envelope he still hadn't opened.

The fire crackled gently behind him, casting golden shadows across the small room. It was a quiet space—bookshelves lined with worn volumes, a globe that had once belonged to his father, and a worn leather chair now occupied by a threadbare scarf draped across the armrest. Scrooge's scarf.

Tim reached out and turned the envelope slowly in his hand.

To Timothy Cratchit – For Christmas Eve. One Last Gift.

The handwriting was unmistakable—precise, deliberate, with a certain elegance that had only come to Scrooge late in life. Tim knew every curve of the letters. He'd once teased the old man about his penmanship improving with redemption.

He traced the edge of the wax seal but didn't break it.

He wasn't sure why.

Maybe it was fear. Maybe reverence.

He had read many letters in his life. But never one from the dead.

Outside, the streetlamps flickered to life, their soft orange halos glowing against the snow that piled on the cobblestones. It was Christmas Eve Eve—the night before everything began to sparkle. The night before the carolers filled the air with songs too old to forget.

Tim looked around the room. It was warm, yes, but too still. The kind of stillness that invited ghosts.

And they came, if not in body, then in memory.

He saw his father, Bob Cratchit, seated beside the hearth, carving a roast too small for seven plates but insisting it was a feast.

He saw his mother humming quietly while sewing patches into Peter's jacket, her fingers swift and sure.

He saw Scrooge standing awkwardly in the doorway one Christmas, unsure whether to knock or simply enter, holding a carved wooden soldier for Tim in one hand and a tin of sweets in the other.

So many ghosts, Tim thought. Not to haunt—but to remind.

He leaned back in the chair and closed his eyes.

It would be easier to give the ledger to someone else. To let the Foundation run itself. Nathan could manage the operations. Grace could keep the accounts. Julia, though still young, had shown promise with her quiet resilience.

But then what? He'd teach until retirement, with the ledger gathering dust on the shelf?

He imagined Scrooge's voice—rough, impatient, but somehow amused.

"You're thinking too small, boy. Always have."

Tim chuckled under his breath. "You always did know when I needed a push."

A knock at the door pulled him from his thoughts.

He hesitated, then rose and opened it.

Nathan stood on the stoop, snow clinging to his shoulders.

"Sorry," he said. "I know it's late."

Tim stepped aside. "Come in."

Nathan entered, rubbing his hands together. "She came back."

Tim blinked. "The girl?"

Nathan nodded. "Sat outside the hall for an hour. Wouldn't come in until I lit the lantern by the door. Said it was the only light she trusted."

Tim poured two cups of tea and handed one to Nathan. "Did she say her name this time?"

"No. But she asked about you again."

Tim took a sip. "Why?"

"She said, 'My mum used to say a Cratchit once saved Christmas. That true?'"

Tim exhaled slowly.

Nathan leaned forward. "You have to see her."

Tim looked at the envelope still lying on the desk, untouched.

"I will," he said quietly. "But not tonight."

Nathan stood. "Tomorrow, then. You've waited long enough."

After he left, Tim returned to the desk.

He picked up the envelope again, studied the seal.

Then he set it down once more—unopened.

Chapter 5

THE SNOW HAD SOFTENED INTO a gentle flurry by morning, the kind that blanketed the city like a secret waiting to be told.

Tim pulled his scarf tighter and stepped through the side gate of the Cratchit Foundation. The old building stood quietly on the corner of Mill and Broad, its windows glowing with the warm light of lanterns already lit inside. A small wreath hung crookedly on the front door, dusted with fresh snow.

Nathan was waiting near the entrance, holding a small ledger of intake notes.

"She's inside," he said, without preamble.

Tim nodded. "Alone?"

"She prefers it. Spoke only once since last night. Said she wasn't supposed to stay long."

"Did she say where she's from?"

Nathan hesitated. "Just that she was running. That someone used to tell her stories about a man who kept Christmas alive."

Tim exhaled slowly. "That sounds like a lie most children wish was true."

Nathan shrugged. "Some lies are just truths that haven't happened yet."

Inside, the front hall smelled of cinnamon, paraffin, and old wood. Bins of donated coats lined the entryway, and the crackle of a distant fireplace hummed in the background.

Tim followed Nathan down the corridor, past the kitchen and the warming room, to a side chamber usually used for tutoring. The door creaked open.

She sat near the window, legs curled beneath her on a frayed cushion, staring out at the falling snow. Her clothes were oversized—borrowed, likely. Her hair, tangled. A small tear ran along the cuff of her coat sleeve.

She turned as they entered. Her eyes were wary, but alert. Intelligent.

Tim approached slowly, pulling a chair over but not yet sitting.

"My name is Tim," he said gently. "May I sit with you?"

She studied him for a moment, then nodded once.

Nathan stepped back quietly and closed the door behind him.

Tim sat, placing his gloved hands in his lap.

"You've asked for me," he said.

She looked away. "You're him. The one my mum used to talk about. Said a Cratchit saved Christmas once, a long time ago."

Tim smiled faintly. "That's a story people like to tell."

"Is it true?"

He looked out the window. "Maybe parts of it are."

She turned back toward him. "My name's Julia."

He blinked, surprised. "That's a beautiful name."

She shrugged, as if unsure whether to accept the compliment. "Mum used to tell stories to help us sleep. Said there was a man who gave things away—not money, but food, warmth. Books. He had a bad leg like mine."

Tim glanced down and saw that her foot was turned slightly inward beneath the cuff of her trousers. The heel of one boot had been unevenly patched.

"And what happened to him in the stories?" he asked.

She shrugged again. "He always showed up. Even when no one thought he would."

Tim felt something shift in his chest. Not sorrow. Not pity.

Recognition.

He cleared his throat. "Would you like to stay for supper tonight? There's music. Sometimes Grace sings."

"I don't sing," she said quickly.

"That's alright. Not everyone has to."

Julia hesitated. "Can I stay in this room?"

Tim smiled. "For as long as you like."

She looked relieved—but also tired. Tired in the way only children who've seen too much too young often are.

Tim stood. "I'll leave the door open, if you're alright with that. And I'll bring you something warm to eat."

"Don't make a fuss," she said, eyes narrowing slightly.

Tim paused, the ghost of a chuckle in his throat. "You sound just like someone I used to know."

As he stepped into the hall, Nathan appeared from around the corner.

"She spoke?"

Tim nodded. "Her name's Julia."

Nathan blinked. "Huh. My mum's name was Julia."

Tim froze.

Then he looked back at the room and said softly, "So was someone else's."

Chapter 6

The ledger sat open on Tim's desk that evening, untouched.

It had been over a week since the funeral, and yet he still hadn't written a single name. Not one. The pages stared back at him like blank verdicts—waiting not just to be filled, but to be earned.

The fire had burned low. Shadows danced against the ceiling in familiar patterns. The same ones that had danced across this room for years while Scrooge sat across from him, grumbling over balance sheets and mumbling about "excessive decimal places."

How could one man leave behind such silence?

Tim rubbed his eyes. Outside, the snow had stopped falling, leaving behind a city painted in stillness. Children would play again tomorrow.

Merchants would reopen. But for now, the night held its breath.

He reached for his tea, now gone cold, and glanced at the envelope again. Still unopened.

He hadn't forgotten it. He couldn't.

But something in him recoiled each time he considered breaking that seal—as though doing so would finalize the loss. That once Scrooge's words were read, they could no longer live in his imagination. They would be finite. Settled.

There was a knock at the door.

He half-expected Nathan again. But when he opened it, he found Grace.

She stood on the stoop with a wrapped bundle in her arms and a knowing look on her face.

"I brought supper," she said, brushing snow off her coat.

"You didn't have to—"

"I never have to," she interrupted. "I choose to. May I come in?"

Tim stepped aside, and Grace entered like she always did—casually, confidently, as though the world were her patient and she its physician. She moved to the kitchen without waiting, setting the bundle on the table.

"I saw her," she said.

"Julia?"

Grace nodded, unwrapping warm bread and soup from under the cloth. "She helped me tidy up the pamphlets this afternoon. Didn't say much. But her hands don't shake as much now."

Tim sat. "She reminds me of someone."

"Yourself?" Grace asked, glancing at him.

"No," he said. "Her."

He nodded toward the mantle, where a small framed sketch of his mother sat between two candles. It was one of the only images that existed of her—done in charcoal by Peter, years ago. Her eyes held patience. Her mouth, gentle defiance.

"She always found the ones no one else saw," he said. "She'd bring home children who'd lost everything and feed them from our own plates, even if it meant she went without."

Grace sat across from him, pouring soup into two bowls. "Sounds like someone else I know."

Tim smiled faintly. "Julia told me her mother used to tell stories about a man who gave away warmth. That he never gave out of pity—only purpose."

Grace handed him a bowl. "And what did you say to that?"

"I told her it was only a story."

Grace paused. "Is it?"

He didn't answer.

They ate in silence for a few minutes, the warmth slowly returning to the room, to their hands, to the unspoken things between them.

Afterward, Grace rose and approached the mantle. She looked down at the envelope.

"You haven't opened it."

Tim shook his head.

"I can't," he admitted. "Not yet."

She studied it, then looked back at him. "Then don't rush. Some gifts don't spoil."

As she moved to leave, she stopped in the doorway.

"She'll ask for more soon," Grace said. "Julia. Not food. Not shelter. But truth."

Tim looked up. "And if I don't have it?"

Grace smiled, warm but unyielding. "Then find it. Or make peace with the silence."

Then she was gone, the door shutting softly behind her.

Tim stared at the envelope.

Then he turned to the ledger, picked up the pen, and for the first time in days, dipped it in ink.

On the blank page he wrote:

Julia — asks nothing but needs everything.

And beneath it:

> *Reminds me that giving isn't always about what we offer... sometimes it's what we endure.*

The ink dried slow.
But it dried.

Chapter 7

THE NEXT MORNING DAWNED GREY and brittle. The sky held the color of old tin, and the frost on the windows turned the panes into lattices of lace.

Tim arrived at the Foundation early, hours before the volunteers. He lit the stove himself, filled the kettle, and checked each of the bins in the warming room. Scarves. Mittens. Coats sorted by size and need. Everything was in place, yet he felt unsettled, like he was waiting for something unseen to shift.

Julia was already there.

She sat on the stairs that led to the upper level, her legs swinging idly, a book open on her lap. Her coat looked slightly neater than yesterday, her hair still a bit tangled but no longer matted. She glanced up but didn't smile.

"You came back," Tim said gently.

She shrugged. "Didn't have anywhere else."

He crossed the room, kneeling down to adjust the flame beneath the stove. "You always have here now."

Julia's voice was quiet. "That's what they said before."

Tim paused. "Who?"

She didn't answer. Instead, she flipped a page in the book—an old copy of Great Expectations missing its cover and half its binding. She ran a finger beneath the words as she read.

"Do you like books?" he asked.

"They don't ask questions," she replied.

Tim sat beside her on the stairs. "Sometimes they do. But only the ones we're ready to answer."

Julia closed the book and hugged it to her chest. "Mum used to read me stories when we couldn't sleep. About magic lanterns. Or angels who wore shoes made of fog."

Tim smiled softly. "Sounds like someone with a gift."

"She said stories kept the dark away. That if I ever found a Cratchit, I should tell them hers weren't all lies."

Tim looked at her for a long moment. "They weren't."

For the first time, her mouth curved just slightly. Not a smile. But something near it.

Grace arrived not long after, bringing boxes of donated goods and a tray of steaming rolls. Nathan followed, whistling as he sorted coats, occasionally slipping a sweet into Julia's pocket when she wasn't looking.

The Foundation buzzed with soft movement—preparation for the Christmas Eve gathering they held every year. Hot soup, carols, warm hands and warmer company. It was the kind of gathering that didn't make headlines but rewrote stories all the same.

By midmorning, Tim found himself at the front desk sorting ledgers. The original one—Scrooge's ledger—remained wrapped in cloth in his satchel. He hadn't brought it out yet.

He wasn't sure it was time.

Julia appeared beside him like a shadow, holding a mug of tea in both hands. "Do you write names?" she asked.

Tim blinked. "Sometimes."

"Why?"

He looked down at the ledger before him—the smaller, daily logbook used for Foundation needs.

"Because names matter," he said. "Because remembering someone can change how we see them."

Julia nodded. "I wrote mine once. In a tunnel. Scratched it into the wall with a nail."

Tim looked up sharply. "A tunnel?"

She nodded. "Under the street. Before we came here."

He didn't ask what she meant by we.

He reached slowly into his satchel and pulled out the leather-bound ledger. It felt heavier in his hands than it ever had before.

He set it gently on the desk, unwrapping it like a sacred object. Julia's eyes widened—not with recognition, but with something close to reverence.

"That's it, isn't it?" she whispered.

Tim nodded. "It belonged to the man who saved me."

"Can I see inside?"

He hesitated. Then turned it toward her and flipped to the page he had written just the night before. Her name stared back at her in black ink.

She read it, blinked, then read it again.

"You wrote me."

"I did."

She was quiet for a long moment.

Then she reached into her pocket and pulled out something small—a scrap of paper, folded four times, nearly crumbling at the edges.

She handed it to him without a word.

He unfolded it slowly. Inside, in careful block letters, were the words:

"When you find the one who sees you, stay."

Tim looked up. Her eyes glistened, but she blinked them clear.
"I think I found him," she said.
Tim said nothing. Only closed the ledger and placed a hand over it, his palm warm against the leather.
"I see you," he said quietly.
And she nodded.

CHAPTER 8

THE SUN BROKE THROUGH FOR the first time in days.

Its light spilled through the upper windows of the Foundation, painting golden rectangles on the worn wood floors and melting patches of snow along the sill. The warmth was weak—but it was enough. Enough to make people pause. Enough to make them smile without knowing why.

Tim stood near the fireplace in the gathering room, reading through a letter delivered that morning. It came from a woman named Eleanor—a widow who had received coal and candles from the Foundation last Christmas. She had included a note that simply read:

> *"You brought light when I had none.*
> *May you always burn brightly."*

He folded it carefully and slipped it into a small leather pouch where he kept such messages—not for accounting, but for remembering.

Across the room, Nathan sorted parcels for the evening event. Grace worked the donation desk, her sleeves rolled up, her brow lightly dusted with flour from the pies she'd brought from home.

Julia sat near the corner of the main room, sorting mittens by size into wooden bins. She was humming. Softly. Almost to herself. But it was unmistakable.

Tim approached with two mugs of tea and handed her one.

"Thank you," she said without looking up.

"You're welcome," he replied. "You're getting very good at this."

"At stacking gloves?"

"At staying," he said gently.

Julia paused mid-stack. Her face didn't move, but her fingers slowed.

"I think my mum would've liked this place," she said.

Tim nodded. "I'm sure she would have."

He crouched beside her and watched her work.

"Would you like to help tonight?" he asked. "The children's table needs someone who can fold paper stars and keep them from dipping their fingers in the custard too early."

Julia's mouth twitched. "That sounds exhausting."

"It is," he said. "Which is why I need someone tough."

She gave him a sideways look. "I'll think about it."

"That's all I ask."

Tim stood and walked back toward the hearth where the donation box had begun to overflow. Mittens, coins, paper notes of gratitude, even a small wooden train carved by someone's grandfather.

He reached for the ledger again.

This time, he wrote:

*Eleanor – wrote by candlelight
to thank a stranger.*

"Kindness remembered is the kind that lasts."

He turned to the next page.
Paused.
Then wrote:

Grace – carries warmth in her sleeves and sense in her spine. Keeps us from drifting."

Nathan – once stole bread. Now gives it away.

He smiled to himself.

The ledger no longer felt heavy. It felt like movement. Like momentum.

That afternoon, he invited Julia to walk with him to the nearby square. She hesitated, then agreed—on the condition they not talk too much.

The snow crunched beneath their boots as they made their way through the market stalls. Vendors were setting up wreaths and lanterns. A group of children practiced their carols on a corner, barely staying in tune but making up for it in volume.

Tim bought them each a ginger biscuit, and they stood by a lamppost, watching the carolers fumble through God Rest Ye Merry, Gentlemen.

Julia tilted her head. "They're awful."

"They're perfect," Tim said.

She smiled. A real one this time.

As they turned to walk back, Julia tugged on his sleeve.

"Will you be here tomorrow night?" she asked.

"Of course."

She looked down. "I don't like crowds. But… I might stay for the stars."

He nodded. "Then I'll save you a paper one."

And for a moment, everything felt still—not like silence, but like peace.

CHAPTER 9

By twilight, the Foundation glowed from within like a lantern in the dark.

Candles flickered along the hallway sills. Garlands of evergreen looped across the wooden beams overhead, each tied with a red ribbon. The scent of cinnamon, melted wax, and freshly baked bread filled the air, mingling with quiet laughter and the rustle of coats being shaken free of snow.

It was the eve of Christmas Eve—Stir-Up Night, some called it. The calm before the feast. The kind of evening that wrapped the world in anticipation.

Tim stood in the main hall, watching Grace arrange the final trays on the long wooden table. Bowls of stew, platters of sweet buns, baskets of apples and oranges, a rare luxury most families hadn't tasted since harvest. There was even a tin of barley sugar twists—donated by a merchant who had once received a kindness from Scrooge in a time of need.

"You've outdone yourself," Tim said.

Grace wiped her hands on her apron. "I was raised by a woman who believed you should always cook like someone unexpected might show up."

He smiled. "You think he will?"

"Scrooge?" She looked toward the empty chair near the hearth—the one no one ever sat in. "I think he never really left."

Tim felt the weight of that settle in his chest. Not as grief. As presence.

Across the room, Nathan was herding a group of children toward the craft tables, where donated paper and colored chalk had been laid out. Julia sat among them, already showing a smaller girl how to fold paper into a star. Her hands moved slowly, deliberately—teaching more than just folding. Teaching calm.

Tim approached as the fire crackled behind them.

"You stayed," he said quietly.

Julia didn't look up. "I said I might."

"Will you come tomorrow night?"

She hesitated. Then: "If there's custard."

He nodded solemnly. "I'll speak to the custard commissioner myself."

One of the younger boys tugged Julia's sleeve. "Show me again?"

She leaned closer, gently taking his hands and guiding the folds.

Tim watched her with quiet awe. How someone so hurt could still offer something so steady. So kind.

He turned back toward the front desk, opened the ledger, and wrote:

> *Julia – folds hope into paper*
> *and hands it to others.*

He paused, then added:

> *"Sometimes the smallest hands*
> *carry the weight of the season."*

The bell above the door jingled, and a woman entered—windblown, red-cheeked, clutching two young boys by the hand. She was wrapped in a blanket, not a coat, and her boots were soaked through. Nathan approached quickly with towels, Grace with a tray of bread.

Tim stood still for a moment, watching it all unfold.

This—this is what Scrooge had built. Not the walls. Not the donations. But the response.

The reflex to help. The instinct to comfort. The impulse to see.

He moved toward the fire and sat in the chair beside the empty one. His knees ached, and the weight of years settled into his shoulders—but so did something else.

Peace.

The warmth in the room wasn't just from the hearth. It was from the people—their stories, their kindness, their presence.

He looked over at Julia, who now laughed—laughed—as a boy tore his paper star and made a joke of it. She didn't scold. She just rolled her eyes and showed him again.

Across the room, Grace hummed as she checked the pot.

Nathan lit another lantern.

The ledger sat open, ready.

And Tim finally felt ready too.

Chapter 10

That night, the snow returned.

It came in soft gusts, sweeping across the rooftops like a sigh, clinging to windows and muffling the world below. London slept under its weight—its chimneys exhaling gently, its lamps haloed in white, its alleys quiet as prayer.

Tim sat alone by the fire.

The Foundation had quieted. The last children had been walked home or tucked into the sleeping loft. Nathan had gone to fetch more coal. Grace had taken Julia with her, promising warm milk and a bedtime story she hadn't told in years.

Now, only Tim remained.

The fire crackled softly, throwing amber light across the floor. Beside him, the ledger sat closed for the first time all day. A half-written entry remained in his thoughts, still forming. He would write it in the morning.

He reached for the envelope again.

Scrooge's envelope.

He held it between his hands for a long moment, feeling the edges with his thumbs. The seal was intact. The paper slightly yellowed at the corners.

His heart beat faster.

And finally—gently—he broke the seal.

Inside was a single sheet, folded once.

No introduction. No farewell. Just Scrooge's familiar script:

> **"*You were never small, my
> boy. Only growing.
> I gave you what I could—but
> you gave it meaning.
> The ledger is yours now. The gift
> is no longer mine to carry.
> Write in it. Or don't.
> Either way, the gift goes on.
> Just promise me one thing:
> See them."***

Tim let the letter rest in his lap.

He closed his eyes.

He remembered being eight years old and sitting on Scrooge's knee in the parlor, reading aloud from a storybook. The old man had pretended not to understand the plot, forcing Tim to explain the moral. Every time, it was the same lesson.

Be kind.

Be brave.

See others.

He opened his eyes and looked around the room.

The paper stars still hung in the window. The boots lined neatly by the door were drying from the snow. The half-finished stack of mittens Julia had sorted remained in its basket, one pair smaller than the rest.

He stood.

Walked to the window.

Outside, the square was empty. But beyond it—beyond the lamplight and frost—he imagined Scrooge walking, cane tapping lightly, humming off-key as he made his rounds in the old days.

Tim smiled.

"You're still here," he whispered.

Then he turned back to the ledger.

Opened it.

And wrote in the margin of the last page:

"I see them."

Then he placed Scrooge's letter inside the front cover, folded carefully like a bookmark, and closed the book.

The fire had burned low. But it had not gone out.

And tomorrow was Christmas Eve.

CHAPTER 11

THE MORNING LIGHT ON CHRISTMAS Eve came gently—no trumpets, no choirs. Just a pale gold seeping through frosted glass, laying soft hands across rooftops, and painting lace shadows on the floorboards of the Foundation.

Tim awoke early.

For the first time in days, he hadn't dreamed. No images of the ledger. No echoes of Scrooge's voice. Just sleep—quiet, uninterrupted, whole.

He stretched slowly, then sat up in the cot tucked into the rear office. It wasn't where he usually slept, but last night had gone late, and the warmth of the fire in the Foundation had felt more welcoming than the silence of his flat.

Across the hallway, he could hear the clink of a teacup and the low hum of Grace's voice.

When he entered the kitchen, she was already there, sleeves rolled, hair pinned back, eyes focused on folding dough for mince pies.

"You're up early," she said without looking.

"You're up earlier," he replied, grabbing a mug from the shelf.

"There's work to do."

"There always is."

She looked at him then. "You slept here?"

He nodded. "Didn't want to miss the morning."

She smiled faintly. "You always were the sentimental one."

He poured tea and sat at the small table by the window. The street outside was still quiet, just the occasional sound of a horse's hooves or a cart wheel crunching over snow.

After a few minutes, Julia padded in.

Her hair was brushed—somewhat. She wore a borrowed wool sweater far too large for her, but it was clean, and it hung from her shoulders like armor.

"Morning," she said, not quite making eye contact.

"Morning," Grace and Tim echoed in unison.

Grace handed her a warm roll. Julia took it and sat opposite Tim without a word.

For several minutes, they ate in silence. No one filled the space with questions or noise. It wasn't necessary.

Then Julia spoke, softly.

"You know, I never had a real Christmas Eve before."

Tim looked up. "No?"

She shook her head. "Sometimes Mum would put a candle in the window. Said it was for the ones who couldn't make it home."

Grace wiped her hands on a towel and leaned against the counter.

"I like that," she said. "A light for someone lost."

Julia nodded. "She used to tell me the world got smaller on Christmas. That if I listened, I might hear people I missed."

Tim smiled, gently. "Your mother was wise."

Julia looked at him. "Do you miss someone today?"

He paused, tea halfway to his lips.

"Yes," he said finally. "More than one."

Julia didn't press.

The fire in the stove snapped, and the clock on the wall ticked steadily forward. Outside, the snow began to fall again—light and slow.

Tim stood and moved toward the back hallway.

"I need to check on the supplies for tonight," he said. "We'll be at capacity."

Grace called after him, "Don't forget the extra candles. You always forget the candles."

"I never forget," he said over his shoulder, smirking.

But he did.

And she knew it.

Later, while checking inventory in the cellar, Tim ran a hand across the stacked crates and marked the remaining tins of soup, biscuits, and wrapped parcels.

The boxes were fewer than years past. Donations had slowed. But the need hadn't.

Still, he wasn't worried.

He had learned something from Scrooge that had stuck deeper than any sermon or lecture: "There is always enough when you start with giving."

He returned upstairs to find Julia stringing popcorn with a sewing needle, sitting in a sunbeam by the window. Grace hummed in the kitchen. Nathan would be arriving soon with more firewood.

It was Christmas Eve.

And they were ready.

Almost.

CHAPTER 12

By early afternoon, the warmth inside the Foundation had become a force of its own.

Children filled the gathering hall, their voices rising and falling in chaotic rhythm. Tables were lined with pies and stew, tins of sweets, paper stars, and folded napkins shaped like holly leaves. Candles flickered in every window. The rooms smelled of cinnamon and cloves, of roasted apples and melted wax.

It was noisy.

It was perfect.

Tim moved through it all like a conductor—quietly keeping rhythm, adjusting trays, slipping mittens onto little hands, straightening a crooked wreath, nodding to Grace as she organized another round of cider.

Nathan had just finished carrying in the last batch of firewood when he motioned to Tim.

"There's someone at the door for you."

Tim frowned. "Who?"

Nathan shrugged. "Didn't say. Bit stiff. Looked like he belonged to the city council or an old ghost story."

Tim stepped into the front hall and opened the door.

A man stood in the snow.

He was tall and spare, wrapped in a wool coat nearly the color of soot. His beard was neatly trimmed. A walking stick rested in his gloved hand. He removed his hat.

"Mr. Cratchit," he said.

Tim nodded slowly. "Yes."

"My name is Howard Winslow. I was… a close associate of Mr. Scrooge."

Tim's eyebrows lifted. "I knew most of his associates."

"Not this kind," the man said.

He stepped inside without waiting to be invited.

Tim shut the door gently behind him. "Go on."

Winslow reached into his coat and removed a small parcel—wrapped in plain brown paper, tied with twine.

"He left this with me. Months ago. Told me to deliver it on Christmas Eve. I was instructed not to open it. Only to hand it to you directly."

Tim took the parcel carefully.

It was light. Unassuming.

Winslow straightened. "He said it was something you'd know what to do with."

Tim glanced up. "And you didn't ask what it was?"

"I learned long ago not to ask Ebenezer Scrooge anything I didn't want a parable in response to."

Tim smiled faintly at that.

Winslow turned to leave, pausing briefly at the threshold.

"I used to think he was mad," he said. "Giving all that away. Living modestly. Spending his time with the poor."

Tim didn't respond.

Winslow looked back. "But maybe madness is what's required to wake a sleeping world."

Then he was gone.

Tim stood in the entryway, the parcel in his hands.

He brought it into the back office and unwrapped it slowly, layer by layer.

Inside was a leather-bound book.

Not the ledger.
A journal.
Scrooge's journal.
Tim opened the first page.
"To Tim, should I not be here to see it through…"
He stopped reading.
Not out of fear this time, but reverence.
He closed the journal and held it tightly.
Another voice to carry forward.
Another chapter to begin.
Outside, the bells of St. Martin's rang for evening service.
Inside, the candles burned brighter, as though they, too, were remembering someone.

Chapter 13

THE BELLS OF ST. MARTIN'S had barely faded when the first carolers appeared at the door.

Their voices, slightly off-key but brimming with heart, drifted through the Foundation's entryway like smoke curling from a chimney. Children clapped. Elders smiled. Grace hurried to light extra lanterns.

Christmas Eve had arrived in full.

Tim stood near the hearth, watching the room fill with life.

There were more people than expected—neighbors from nearby streets, families bundled in wool, solitary figures drawn by the promise of warmth. Some came for food. Others for company. A few, perhaps, for something they didn't yet know they needed.

Julia helped pour cider, her movements measured but confident. She no longer clung to corners. She met eyes now. She smiled—once, even at Nathan, who had slipped a ribbon into her pocket when she wasn't looking.

Grace moved through the crowd like she'd been born to host banquets. She tied scarves, refilled trays, laughed easily, and somehow kept the custard from being touched until the right moment.

Tim felt none of it slipping past him. He absorbed every detail.

At one point, Martha arrived—older, yes, but with the same quick wit. She greeted Tim with a kiss on the cheek and handed him a wrapped loaf of gingerbread "for when the saints forget to bring dessert."

He laughed.

And he felt, deeply, the presence of those no longer with them.

His parents. Scrooge.

Even the city felt different tonight. Not quieter, but softer. Willing, for once, to listen.

When the carols paused and the children quieted, Grace approached Tim with a gentle touch on the elbow.

"They're ready for your reading," she said.

He nodded and stepped to the front of the hall. A hush settled. Candles flickered in the windows. The fire glowed behind him, steady and low.

Tim held the ledger—not Scrooge's journal, but the ledger itself—in his hands. Its spine was worn. The edges frayed. But it still carried its weight with dignity.

He looked out at the crowd.

"I was given this book many years ago," he began. "Not as a gift, exactly—but as a responsibility."

He ran a hand along the cover.

"It contains names. Not of kings or generals. But of people who gave, and people who received. Acts of kindness. Moments of mercy. Some of the names you'd recognize. Others you wouldn't."

He flipped to a page.

"I'd like to read one."

He cleared his throat.

**"Eleanor – wrote by candlelight to thank a stranger.

'Kindness remembered is the kind that lasts.'"**

He closed the book gently.

"Tonight, we write new names. In our hearts, if not in ink. We become part of something older than ourselves. We remember what it means to see one another—and to be seen."

Silence followed. Not awkward. Sacred.

Then the youngest caroler—a boy with flushed cheeks and a lopsided crown made of paper—began to sing:

"Silent night… holy night…"

The others joined, and soon the whole room filled with song.

Tim stood with the ledger at his side, surrounded by voices and light.

And for the first time in many winters, he felt something he hadn't allowed himself to feel:

Joy.

Not the loud kind.

The deep kind. The kind that hums through your ribs like a remembered lullaby.

Chapter 14

The fire had burned low again.

Most of the guests had gone. A few lingered outside the doors, saying goodbyes beneath drifting snowflakes. Candles flickered along the windowsills. The music had stopped. Only the soft clatter of dishes from the back kitchen broke the stillness.

Tim sat alone at the long table, hands resting on the closed ledger, eyes half-lidded in the glow of the hearth.

Across the room, Julia swept stray crumbs from the floor with a small broom. She moved slowly, as if stretching out the task so the moment wouldn't end.

"You don't have to do that," Tim said.

Julia didn't look up. "I know."

He watched her a moment longer, then gestured toward the bench beside him. "Sit?"

She hesitated, then set the broom aside and crossed the room.

They sat in silence for a while, the fire warming their faces.

Tim finally broke it. "Did you enjoy tonight?"

Julia nodded. "More than I thought I would."

"You were wonderful with the children."

"I didn't do much."

"You did more than you know."

She looked at the ledger on the table. "Is it heavy?"

Tim smiled faintly. "Some days, yes."

"Do you ever want to stop?"

He didn't answer right away.

"I don't know if stopping is allowed," he said finally. "Not when you've been given this much."

Julia looked down at her hands. "I'm afraid of being seen."

"I was too," Tim said. "For years."

"What changed?"

"Someone looked anyway. And didn't flinch."

She absorbed that.

Then asked, "When did you stop being 'Tiny'?"

Tim chuckled softly. "When I realized I didn't have to fit the name people gave me."

She looked over at him.

"I don't think I'm brave enough to carry something like that," she said, glancing at the ledger.

"You don't have to carry it," Tim replied. "You just have to continue it."

The fire popped. Outside, a gust of wind shook loose a drift of snow from the eaves.

Tim turned slightly toward her. "Do you want to write something in it?"

Julia blinked. "Me?"

He nodded. "You saw them too tonight. The people who needed remembering."

She hesitated, then reached out slowly and placed her fingertips on the cover.

"What if I ruin it?"

"You won't," he said. "The only way to ruin it… is to ignore it."

She swallowed hard, then opened to a blank page.

The pen rested nearby. She picked it up, hands trembling slightly, and wrote:

*"Hannah – laughed for the
first time after soup."*

Then underneath, smaller:

"I think she forgot to be afraid."

She set the pen down and stared at the page.

Tim watched her carefully, saying nothing.

After a moment, Julia spoke, barely above a whisper.

"My mum's name was Hannah."

Tim nodded. "Then maybe tonight was for both of you."

She leaned back against the bench, staring into the fire.

"I don't know what happens next," she said.

"None of us do," Tim replied. "But now you're part of it."

Julia smiled—small and quiet.

But real.

Chapter 15

THE FOUNDATION HAD FALLEN SILENT.

It was well past midnight now. The candles had burned low, and most of the lanterns had been extinguished. Outside, the snow had settled into soft drifts along the edges of the walk, blanketing the street in white.

Tim remained by the fire.

He had returned to the hearth after helping Grace settle the last of the dishes and seeing the final families out. Nathan had left an hour ago, waving sleepily and promising to be back before dawn with bread for Christmas morning.

Julia had fallen asleep upstairs in the small loft, wrapped in two blankets and surrounded by folded paper stars.

Tim sat in Scrooge's old chair—the one everyone still refused to sit in, even after all these years.

It creaked slightly as he leaned back, resting the ledger in his lap.

He didn't write.

Not yet.

Instead, he just listened.

To the fire.

To the clock.

To the stillness that followed joy.

Grace entered quietly, carrying two mugs of mulled cider. She handed one to him, then settled into the armchair opposite.

"Your eyes are red," she said gently.

Tim nodded. "I read the journal."

She said nothing.

He took a slow sip.

"It wasn't instructions," he said. "It wasn't even guidance. Just… stories. Small moments. Bits of thought. Things he remembered and never said out loud."

Grace smiled. "Sounds like him."

"He was lonelier than I realized," Tim said. "Even after he changed."

"He'd lived alone too long," she said. "Even good men forget how to be known."

Tim looked into the fire. "He didn't believe in legacies. Not the grand kind. But he kept writing anyway. He thought if his hands were moving, maybe he wouldn't vanish."

"You're not vanishing," Grace said softly.

He turned to her. "Aren't I?"

She shook her head. "You're planting."

They sat in silence again, the flames casting tall shadows on the wall.

"I think she could carry it," Tim said quietly.

He nodded. "Not yet. Maybe not for a while. But someday."

Grace leaned forward. "She already is."

Tim looked down at the ledger. "I thought I had to protect it. Preserve it. But maybe I was just afraid to let it evolve."

Grace's voice was calm. "You didn't fail him."

"I know," Tim said. "But I don't want to fail her."

"You won't."

They sipped their cider slowly. Outside, the snow continued to fall, and a nearby clock tower chimed once, twice—marking the last few hours of Christmas Eve.

Tim looked to the fire again.

"She wrote her mother's name in the ledger," he said.

Grace raised an eyebrow. "Did she?"

"She didn't say it. But I know."

He opened the book and read the line again.

"Hannah – laughed for the first time after soup. I think she forgot to be afraid."

Grace smiled, her eyes soft.

"That's how you know the ledger's in good hands," she said.

Tim nodded, fingers resting gently on the edge of the page.

"I think," he whispered, "this might be my last Christmas with it."

Grace looked at him for a long time. "Are you ready to let it go?"

Then: "Not yet. But I'm ready to prepare someone else to hold it."

Chapter 16

Christmas morning arrived quietly.

No trumpets, no clamor. Just the soft hush of snowfall and the faint aroma of cinnamon and ash from a fire that had burned through the night.

Tim awoke in the chair near the hearth, a blanket draped over his legs, the ledger still resting gently against his chest.

For a moment, he forgot what day it was.

Then he heard the laughter.

It wasn't loud. Not wild. Just a child's burst of joy echoing down the stairs like a warm ripple in still water.

He smiled before opening his eyes.

When he finally stood, stretching slowly, he moved toward the hallway and saw Julia at the base of the stairs, holding a small tray of oranges.

Grace was beside her, whispering something with a grin, and Julia nodded—barely, but she nodded.

"Morning," Tim said, his voice still thick with sleep.

Julia turned. "You're late."

Tim chuckled. "You started without me?"

"We had to," Grace said. "The custard wouldn't wait."

He moved toward the kitchen and saw the table set again—simpler this time. No guests. No crowd. Just bowls of stew, warm bread, and gifts wrapped in butcher paper and twine.

Nathan arrived a few minutes later, brushing snow from his shoulders and carrying a basket of apples so full it nearly burst.

"I was mugged by a caroler," he said. "Refused to let me pass until I joined the chorus."

"Did you?" Grace asked.

"I did. She was six. I had no chance."

Julia laughed—soft, but unmistakable.

They gathered around the table, plates filled, cider poured. The morning passed without ceremony. Just smiles. Just conversation. Just warmth.

Tim didn't speak much.

He listened.

Watched.

Noticed.

The way Julia now leaned into Grace without bracing for disappointment. The way Nathan poured cider for others before himself. The way Grace looked over the room not with stress, but with something like pride.

After breakfast, the four of them sat near the fire. The ledger remained closed on the table.

Julia picked it up slowly.

"Can I add one more?" she asked.

Tim nodded.

She turned to a fresh page and wrote carefully:

> *"Nathan – sings when cornered,*
> *feeds everyone else first."*

Then, without lifting her pen, she added:

> *"Grace – makes homes from*
> *rooms and steadies storms."*

She looked at Tim.

"You're already in here," she said. "But I think there's more."

He leaned forward. "What do you mean?"

She turned to a blank page and wrote a final line:

"Tim – doesn't let go. Not until he's certain someone else can hold on."

He stared at the words for a long moment. And didn't stop her.

Chapter 17

The city square was alive with color by midday.

Lanterns hung from gaslights, wreaths looped around balcony rails, and great banners fluttered from buildings declaring "A Season of Grace. A Spirit of Giving." Snow still dusted the cobblestones, but it had thinned enough for people to move freely without slipping into one another's arms—though some did anyway, by choice or chance.

Tim stood near the back of the crowd.

He hadn't planned to attend the mayor's Christmas proclamation. The Foundation had never been much for spectacle. But Nathan had insisted. And Grace had given him that look—that subtle, unmistakable tilt of the head that meant, *you're going, and I won't hear a word about it.*

Now, he watched quietly as the mayor—a round man in a tailored coat—adjusted his spectacles and raised his gloved hands.

"This year," the mayor said, "we acknowledge a quiet revolution in our city. One that began not in parliament, nor palace, but in a cold counting house many years ago… and was continued by those who knew its worth."

Tim's eyebrows lifted.

He hadn't expected to be named.

The mayor gestured behind him, and two uniformed workers unveiled a bronze plaque set into a stone pedestal.

Carved across its surface:

"The Cratchit Foundation – Established in Kindness, Maintained by Grace."

In honor of Ebenezer Scrooge and Timothy Cratchit – givers of second chances.

There was a smattering of applause. Then more. Then more still.

Tim stood frozen.

He had never asked for this. Never sought his name in stone.

He turned slightly and saw Julia at his side. Her eyes were wide.

"They put you on a plaque," she whispered.

He nodded once. "Apparently so."

"Is that… weird?"

He smiled. "A bit."

Grace came up beside them, linking arms with Julia.

"They asked me if they should do it," she whispered. "I said you'd pretend to hate it but secretly be honored."

He chuckled.

As the crowd dispersed, small groups came to offer thanks. A baker whose child had been fed in the winter of '89. A seamstress whose sister had lived upstairs at the Foundation. A boy, now grown, who had once received a pair of mittens and remembered the smell of the stew more than the meal itself.

Tim listened.

He accepted their words, their gratitude, and their stories.

But he didn't step up to the plaque.

He didn't need to.

As the square thinned out, he turned to Julia.

"How did it feel, seeing it?" he asked.

She considered. "Big."

"You don't need a plaque," he said gently. "You just need a page."

She looked at him. "Can I write mine?"

He nodded.

And together, they stepped away from the crowd.

Toward the next blank space in the book.

CHAPTER 18

They returned to the Foundation just as the sun dipped behind the rooftops.

The gold of the sky faded into lavender. Streetlamps buzzed to life. Snow crunched underfoot but no longer fell. The city exhaled slowly—its day ending, its heart still beating.

Tim unlocked the door with the brass key he had carried for nearly two decades.

The same key Scrooge had once handed him in silence.

Julia stepped in behind him. She didn't speak. She no longer needed to.

Inside, the warmth returned at once. The fire Grace had lit before leaving still glowed in the hearth. A basket of folded coats sat neatly by the door. The scent of tea leaves lingered in the air.

Tim walked to the desk and unwrapped the ledger from its cloth covering.

He laid it flat on the table, then stepped back.

Julia approached and stood beside him.

Tim looked at her—not as a child, not as a guest—but as something more.

"Would you like to try leading tomorrow's gathering?"

She blinked. "Me?"

He nodded. "The children's hour. The carols. The cider. I'll be nearby. But I want them to look to you."

Julia hesitated. "What if I forget what to say?"

"Then you'll listen instead."

"And if I mess it up?"

"You won't," he said softly. "But even if you do… the gift forgives."

She nodded slowly.

Tim pulled out a folder of the following day's roster—food distribution, arrival times, firewood supply, volunteer names. He handed it to her.

"Start here," he said. "You don't need to do it all. But I want you to know how it works."

She sat down and opened the folder like it was a spellbook.

Tim stood back, watching her eyes scan the pages, her fingers tracing the lines.

He turned away and walked to the window, gazing out into the city beyond.

He had carried the ledger through wars and winters, through times of famine and feast, through doubt and joy.

But nothing had prepared him for the feeling of relief that came with placing part of it in someone else's hands.

Not because he was finished.

But because someone else was beginning.

He whispered, as if to himself, "She sees them."

Behind him, Julia's voice rose, quiet but clear.

"Tim?"

He turned.

She held up the ledger.

"Do I add your name again?"

He smiled.

"No," he said. "Just leave space."

CHAPTER 19

Tim moved slower now.

He noticed it in the way the stairs felt steeper, the tea took longer to steep, and the cold reached deeper into his bones. But he didn't resent it. Not anymore. He'd stopped trying to outrun time and instead had learned to walk beside it.

The Foundation had entered a quiet stretch between the holidays. The frenzy of Christmas had passed, but the need remained—the cold didn't yield to the calendar.

He stood in the back office, organizing donation records, sorting gloves into their correct boxes, rereading the messages left on the "Gratitude Tree" from Christmas Eve. A child's crayon scrawl caught his eye:

"Thank you for warm hands and songs."

He smiled and tucked it inside the ledger as a bookmark.

He hadn't written in it for three days.

Not because he had nothing to say—but because Julia had.

He had watched her take quiet charge of the children's gathering the day before, calmly organizing crafts and helping serve cider with steady hands. She didn't speak often, but when she did, the room listened.

She was becoming someone.

And not someone new.

Someone true.

Tim stepped out into the hallway and made his usual rounds. He stopped at the pantry, checked the bin of kindling, refilled the tea jar. He wasn't needed—but he was still useful. That mattered.

He paused in front of the mirror in the foyer—a tall rectangle with an iron frame, gifted by a benefactor years ago. He studied his reflection.

His hair had thinned. His shoulders stooped. The lines beside his eyes had deepened.

But the boy who had once limped through the snow on Scrooge's arm still lived in there. Still blinked behind the older eyes. Still believed.

Behind him, the door creaked open.

Julia stepped in, cheeks pink from the cold, mittens stuffed in her coat pockets.

"Coal delivery's late," she said. "I'll keep watch."

He turned. "You don't have to do that."

"I know," she said, heading to the window seat. "But I want to."

He watched her settle in with the ledger on her lap, flipping through pages with the ease of someone who knew them now—not as history, but as inheritance.

Tim walked slowly back to the office.

He sat at his desk.

And this time, he opened the journal Scrooge had left him.

He flipped through the familiar handwriting, pausing at a line he had underlined months ago but hadn't spoken aloud until now:

> *"The gift only survives when*
> *it changes hands."*

Tim whispered it to himself. Then again. Then again.

Then he picked up a blank piece of paper and wrote:

"I think she's ready."

GARY J. ROSE

He folded it and tucked it between the pages.
And for the first time in his life, he felt lighter.
Not empty.
Ready.

Chapter 20

Winter softened its grip by the time February arrived.

The snow came less often. The wind, though still biting, no longer howled with the same bitterness. Icicles melted from the eaves in the mid-morning sun, and the air began to smell faintly of earth beneath the frost.

Tim's steps had slowed, but his mind had not. He still rose early. Still lit the lamps before the others arrived. Still knew how many mittens were left in the blue bin and how many names had been added to the ledger since the new year.

But he no longer held the pen.

Not every day.

More often now, he found Julia already seated by the window with the book open, entries written in her careful, deliberate hand.

Today was one of those days.

He found her there, wrapped in the same oversized sweater she'd arrived in months ago—though now it looked like it belonged to her. She was adding a name when he entered. She didn't hear him at first.

"Thomas – sang even when no one was listening."

When she noticed him, she closed the book and looked up. "Is this what it's supposed to feel like?"

"What?"

"This… peace."

He crossed the room slowly and sat beside her.

"I think so," he said. "Or at least, this is the closest we ever get."

She rested the pen across the edge of the book. "You didn't sleep at the Foundation last night."

"No," Tim said. "I stayed home. First time in a long while."

"Did it feel strange?"

"Yes. And… right."

Julia studied him a moment. "You're not leaving, are you?"

He shook his head. "I'm not going anywhere. But I am… stepping back. Letting the gift breathe without my hands on it."

She nodded, absorbing it.

"I'm not scared," she said.

"I know," Tim replied. "That's how I knew you were ready."

They sat in silence, the fire humming in the hearth.

After a while, she opened the ledger and turned to the final blank page.

"Would you like to write the last one?" she asked.

Tim shook his head gently. "No. That one belongs to you."

Julia picked up the pen.

She hesitated for only a moment.

Then she wrote:

> *"Tim – never stopped believing the world could be better. Even when it wasn't."*

And beneath that:

> *"He made Christmas last longer than a season."*

She set the pen down and closed the book.

Tim reached out, placed a hand over hers.

"Thank you," he whispered.

She leaned her head against his shoulder.

They sat like that until the fire dimmed.

Outside, the first crocus of spring pushed its head through the snow.

CHAPTER 21

Tim awoke in the middle of the night to the sound of wind rattling the shutters.

He sat upright, heart racing, though there'd been no storm in the forecast. The hearth had gone cold. Moonlight spilled across the floorboards in long silver ribbons, and the shadows in the corners of the room looked somehow thicker than they should.

He rose slowly, pulling his robe tight.

Then he saw it.

A figure stood by the fireplace.

It was cloaked in pale gray, almost silver, and though its face was shrouded, its presence was unmistakable.

Tim didn't need a name.

"I know you," he said quietly. "You were the one who showed him… the grave."

The Spirit of Christmas Yet to Come did not speak. It never had.

It lifted one hand—white, gloved, still—and gestured toward the window.

Tim followed.

Outside, the city shimmered not with snow but with silence. He saw London as if from above—its rooftops distant and shrouded in mist. But it wasn't the city he knew.

There were no lanterns in the square. No carolers. The windows of the Cratchit Foundation were dark. The building was shuttered.

The streets were empty. Except for the children.

Tim watched them huddle in doorways, rag-wrapped and hollow-eyed. One boy carried a broken sign that read *"HOPE"*—but the letters had faded to nothing.

He turned. The figure pointed again.

Now Tim stood in a room he didn't recognize. A council chamber. Familiar voices echoed from the shadows—men debating whether to allocate funds for heating or wall plaques.

Someone mentioned the foundation, called it "a quaint relic."

Another voice, one he could not place, laughed and said, "That was Cratchit's thing, wasn't it? He meant well, but it never lasted."

Tim clenched his fists.

The Spirit's hand moved again.

A graveyard.

Tim stepped forward, afraid.

He saw the stone before he read it.

His own name.

Timothy Cratchit – Remembered briefly, forgotten longer

He dropped to his knees.

"No."

The Spirit did not move.

"I won't let this happen," Tim whispered. "Not to them. Not to us."

He looked up.

The graveyard faded.

So did the council chamber. The street. The Spirit.

Tim stood once more in his parlor, heart pounding, the moonlight exactly where it had been.

The fire remained cold, but the shutters had stilled.

He crossed to the desk and pulled open the ledger.

He turned to a blank page.

What I saw was not prophecy, but warning. What fades must be tended. What fails must be lifted.

He closed the book and placed it gently on the table.

Then, for the first time in weeks, he relit the fire.

It burned brighter than before.

Chapter 22

THE FIRST TIME JULIA ASKED if she could write something, Grace assumed she meant a letter.

"Not just a note," the girl clarified, eyes serious. "Something... people can read. Something that stays."

Grace blinked, then smiled. "What did you have in mind?"

"A story," Julia said. "About people like me."

They began working on it in the evenings after the presses stopped. Grace would review grammar and layout, while Julia chose the words. She didn't write like a child. Her sentences were simple, but they burned.

Tim read the first draft in silence. When he reached the final line, he set the page down, stood, and hugged her.

Julia didn't pull away.

They titled it *"What I Know About the Cold."*

The editorial ran in the Sunday edition of the East End Register.

It wasn't long. Barely four paragraphs.

But it was shared. Clipped. Read aloud in council meetings and church halls. One family posted it in their bakery window. Another tacked it to the church door.

Some cried. Some donated. A few brought food to the foundation doorstep without saying a word.

The editorial read, in part:

> *"I know what it's like to pretend you're not hungry because you don't want your mum to cry. I know what it's like to have no coat and pretend you don't feel the cold. And I know what it's like when someone finally sees you—not as a problem or a number, but as a girl who still wants to grow up."*

> *"I don't want pity. I want you to believe that someone like me can still become someone like you. Or better."*

It ended simply: *"We're still here. We're still cold. But we're watching."*

After its publication, Julia received her first letter.

It came from a girl in Manchester who wrote:

"I thought I was the only one."

Grace found Julia crying quietly after reading it.

"You did that," she whispered.

The next day, Grace and Tim helped Julia pin the original manuscript to the back wall of the foundation, above the ledgers.

Tim added an entry:

**Julia – no longer just a name.
Now a voice. One they can't ignore.**

Then he picked up a pen and wrote across the top of a new page:

Future Projects: Outreach through story.

Below it, one more line:

**The cold can be endured.
What saves us is the warmth of words.**

CHAPTER 23

NATHAN HAD NEVER BEEN MUCH for speeches.

But that spring morning, he stood before the gathered volunteers of the Cratchit Foundation, palms sweating, a folded paper trembling slightly in his hand. Julia stood at his side, holding a stack of printed brochures she had helped design. Grace gave him a subtle nod from the back of the room. Tim waited patiently in the front row.

Nathan cleared his throat.

"I've been working on something," he began. "A way to take what we do here… and carry it forward. Beyond us. Beyond this building."

He held up the paper.

"We call it the Ledger of Tomorrow."

He explained: a new initiative to place ledgers—simplified versions—into local schools, youth centers, and churches. Each book would include stories of kindness, service, and small miracles. But more importantly, students would be encouraged to write their own entries. Acts of compassion. Moments of courage. Names that mattered to them.

"It won't be just a book," Nathan said. "It'll be a living memory. A mirror for the next generation to see the impact they can have."

There was silence at first.

Then applause.

Tim stood and approached him.

"It's brilliant," he said. "You've found the next chapter."

Nathan exhaled. "You really think so?"

Tim placed a hand on his shoulder. "I know so."

Later that day, Nathan and Julia walked to the first school participating in the program. They delivered the inaugural copy—bound in soft leather, with the Cratchit crest embossed in gold on the front.

On the inside cover, in careful ink, it read:

> ***This ledger belongs to those who care enough to change something. Use it well.***

The principal thanked them both and promised to begin using it in class that very week.

As they left, Julia asked, "Do you think kids will really write in it?"

Nathan smiled. "If they're anything like us, they'll write more than we ever imagined."

That evening, Tim made his own entry.

Nathan – once nearly lost, now a guidepost.

Ledger of Tomorrow – the past gives us tools. The future gives us purpose.

He stared at the flame in the hearth, watching it dance and twist. So much had changed. But the heart of it—names written in love, in hope, in remembrance—remained.

The work would outlive them all.

And that, Tim thought, was exactly how it should be.

Chapter 24

THE SNOW RETURNED JUST IN time.

It dusted the rooftops and softened the gaslight glow in the square. Lanterns flickered like stars brought down to earth, and laughter echoed off the stones as children chased each other in scarves too long and boots too big.

Inside the Cratchit Foundation, the first Christmas Banquet was already underway.

Tim stood near the entrance, watching as guests filtered in—some with fancy hats and warm coats, others with patched jackets and shy glances. All were welcome. That was the rule. That had always been the rule.

Tables lined the room, each one decorated with paper stars cut by schoolchildren and small bundles of holly tied with string. Julia had designed the menu herself—roast goose, of course, along with stewed apples, warm bread, and a sweet pudding she'd insisted came from her late mother's recipe.

Grace manned the kitchen with a team of volunteers.

Nathan and Peter stood near the coat rack, laughing as they tried to organize the chaos of donations and misplaced mittens.

The new "Ledger of Tomorrow" sat open on a pedestal by the tree.

Children had already added entries—some in scribbles, others in careful cursive.

"Gave my blanket to Sam because his was torn."

"Helped Mum carry water."

"Told my sister I love her even though she steals my sweets."

Tim read each one like scripture.

Later that evening, he stepped forward to say a few words.

"I won't keep you long," he began. "I just wanted to thank you—for being part of something that started with a name. My name. Written down by a man who decided not to look away."

He paused, eyes glistening.

"And now your names are here. In this room. In that ledger. In each other's hearts. That's how we keep the light going."

There was no grand applause. Just quiet nods, raised glasses, and warm smiles.

After dessert, the tree was lit.

Children gasped. Adults chuckled. The lights weren't perfect—some flickered—but it didn't matter.

The moment did.

Tim wandered to the back of the room as the music began. He sat by the fireplace, removed a slim, cloth-bound book from his coat, and opened to the final page.

One last entry.

"Legacy is not a thing we leave behind. It is the warmth we pass forward. Like candles from hand to hand."

He closed the book.

Outside, the snow fell gently.

And for once, the world did not feel heavy.

It felt light.

Like the first breath of morning on Christmas Day.

He looked over the room, raised his glass again, and said with gentle clarity:

"As I said once before…
God bless us, every one."

Chapter 25

THE WIND HOWLED AGAINST THE shutters like an old ghost denied entry. The fire had dwindled to embers, and Tim sat still in the worn chair, a blanket draped over his knees, Scrooge's ledger resting heavy on his lap. He had not written in it tonight. He had not written at all.

The letter from Peter remained folded on the mantle, unopened. The latest from the school had been worse—Nathan's apprenticeship was in jeopardy after a patron complained about his "criminal record." The council was backpedaling. Support was evaporating. The gift, it seemed, was growing cold.

Tim stared into the ashes, where only the faintest glow remained.

He whispered aloud, "I've failed."

Then the room grew colder.

It wasn't the draft from the window, nor the dying fire. It was something else. Something weightier, older. The air grew thick, dense with memory.

Tim looked up.

A figure stood in the doorway. Not shadow, not light. Something in between.

His breath caught.

"Father?"

Bob Cratchit stepped into the room, his face as kind and familiar as it had ever been—hair thinner, coat worn, eyes soft with that perpetual patience he had always carried like a second skin. He looked as he had in those final years, when the children were mostly grown but still needed him more than they admitted.

Tim blinked, expecting the vision to dissolve. But it didn't.

"Is this… real?" he asked quietly.

Bob tilted his head, the hint of a smile playing on his lips. "Real enough for what you need."

Tim's throat tightened. "I must be dreaming."

"Likely," Bob said gently. "But dreams are sometimes the only place we hear the truth we already know."

Tim wanted to speak, but the words stuck.

Bob took a step closer and looked around the room, nodding as if in approval. "You've done well. Better than I imagined."

"No," Tim said. "I tried. But the city doesn't care. The ledger isn't enough. And I... I'm not enough."

Bob frowned, and for the first time, his voice carried a sharper edge. "Don't you dare."

Tim blinked.

"Don't you dare diminish what you've done," Bob continued. "You think I never felt that way? That I didn't come home from the counting house some nights wondering how I'd make it to the next?"

Tim shook his head. "But you had faith. You had—"

"I had you," Bob interrupted. "And your sisters. And your mother. I had reason. Even when I had nothing else. And you... have reason, Tim. You always have."

Tim swallowed hard. "It doesn't feel like it."

Bob sat on the hearth, the way he used to when Tim was small and coughing and couldn't sleep. "You remember that winter—the one after the fever?"

Tim nodded. "I couldn't walk without pain for months."

"And yet, you insisted on helping with the coal. You dragged that scuttle to the stove every morning, shaking with the effort."

"I wanted to feel useful."

Bob smiled. "You were useful. Not because of the coal. Because you never stopped trying."

Tim looked down at his hands, the ledger balanced between them. "I'm so tired, Father."

"I know." Bob's tone softened again. "But listen to me—this is what the ledger means. It's not just names and gifts and good intentions. It's faith recorded. It's a trail of hope someone else can follow."

Tim glanced at the closed curtains, the windows fogged with frost. "What if I can't finish it?"

Bob stood slowly. "Then you pass it on. You train their hearts like I tried to train yours. Not in arithmetic or scripture. But in kindness. In what it means to lift someone quietly, when no one else is watching."

Tim met his gaze, eyes wet. "I miss you."

"I never left," Bob said. "You carry me. In every page of that book. In every name you write."

Silence filled the room again. Not heavy. Sacred.

Then Bob turned, stepping toward the shadow of the hallway. He looked back only once.

"You were never Tiny," he said. "You were always Tim. That's who changed the world."

And he was gone.

No shimmer. No flash of light. Only the return of ordinary night sounds—the soft tick of the mantle clock, the crackle of a lone ember.

Tim stared at the empty hearth, his chest rising with a long breath.

He opened the ledger.

And in the margin beside the last entry, he wrote:

> *"Visited by the past. Strengthened for the future. The gift is not over."*

Then he rose, stepped to the window, and pulled the curtains aside.

Outside, snow had begun to fall again.

Soft, silent, steady.

Tim watched it for a while.

Then he whispered, "Thank you."

And for the first time in weeks, he felt warm.

Chapter 26

IT WAS THE LONGEST NIGHT of the year.

The sort of Christmas Eve when the cold slipped under doors and behind shutters, when even the gas lamps flickered nervously in the wind. London had wrapped itself in fog and frost, and the bells of St. Martin's rang like distant memories through the snow-stilled streets.

Tim remembered it as clearly as yesterday.

He had been no more than eleven, his gait still unsteady, his voice still boyish and thin. It was the second Christmas after Scrooge had changed, and though the man's transformation was the stuff of whispered astonishment among shopkeepers and chimney sweeps, to the Cratchits he had already become something more permanent—unpredictable, yes, but undeniably present.

That night, just after supper, Scrooge arrived in an enormous wool coat and a scarf so long it trailed like a tail. His cheeks were red, his eyes bright, and his arms were full of parcels wrapped in plain brown paper.

"I need your help," he had said to Tim, who had been curled up beside the hearth.

"With what?"

"Delivery."

Tim blinked. "Now?"

Scrooge leaned in. "It must be tonight. That's when the magic works best."

Martha raised an eyebrow. "You'll have him catching his death—"

"Bah," Scrooge muttered, but with a grin. "The boy's stronger than all of us."

And so they set out.

Tim wore three layers beneath his coat, and Scrooge had tied the scarf around his neck twice for good measure. They moved like shadows through the alleys of Camden and Clerkenwell, Scrooge checking addresses scrawled on a folded sheet while Tim carried the bundles in a sack nearly as big as he was.

They knocked on no doors.

Instead, they left parcels on stoops, tucked behind boots, or nestled inside cracked mail slots. Each one contained something different—

warm mittens, tins of sweets, a loaf of bread, a secondhand book with the nameplate carefully scratched out.

Tim hadn't asked where the names had come from, but he had noticed most of the addresses were in neighborhoods where the fog seemed thicker and the gas lamps less reliable.

"Who are they for?" he had asked once, after leaving a wrapped scarf on a stoop with broken steps.

"People like you," Scrooge had replied.

Tim glanced up. "Crippled?"

"No," Scrooge said, and his voice was gentler than Tim expected. "People who once thought no one saw them."

They continued in silence for a while.

Later, they passed a family sleeping beneath a bridge, curled together in blankets that looked more like rags. Scrooge paused, rummaged in his coat, and handed Tim the last parcel—a simple tin of shortbread.

"No address?" Tim asked.

Scrooge pointed. "Deliver it."

Tim approached carefully, knelt beside the smallest child, and left the tin within arm's reach. As he rose, the child stirred, opening one eye.

"Are you an angel?" the boy asked.

Tim's breath caught. "No. Just… passing through."

The boy smiled faintly and rolled back into sleep.

Back on the street, Scrooge said nothing for several blocks.

Then, in front of an old bakery with frosted windows, he stopped. "You were once that boy," he said. "And now you're the one giving."

Tim looked up at him. "Why does it matter?"

"Because," Scrooge said, placing a hand on his shoulder, "you'll remember this long after I'm gone. And one day, when someone asks you why you believe in second chances, you'll tell them about this night."

They didn't speak again until they returned to the Cratchit home, where the fire had burned low but the room still held warmth.

Scrooge handed Tim the empty sack.

"That's it?" Tim asked.

"For tonight," Scrooge said. "But the giving doesn't stop. It only changes hands."

And with that, he departed into the swirling snow, his scarf flapping behind him like a banner of some new, quiet army.

Tim never forgot that night.

Not because of the cold. Not because of the gifts.

But because, for the first time, he had seen giving not as obligation—but as magic.

Even now, decades later, he could still feel the weight of that sack, the tingle in his fingers, the breath of the child beneath the bridge.

And the one that lit every one to follow.

Chapter 27

THE FIRST TIME JULIA SPOKE aloud in Grace's presence, it was with a whisper that barely rose above the rustling of paper.

It had been nearly two months since she arrived at the print shop with nothing but a crumpled note and a vacant stare. Grace had given her food, a cot in the back room, and something far more important—space. The girl worked in silence, sorting flyers, cleaning rollers, folding stacks with careful precision. She asked for nothing. She refused everything that made her visible.

Until that afternoon.

The machines had fallen quiet, and Grace was working on a new handbill—a notice for a winter clothing drive sponsored by the Cratchit Fund. Julia was seated nearby, cutting twine, when she suddenly looked up.

"May I write something for the flyer?"

Grace turned slowly. Not because she was surprised the girl could speak—but because the girl had chosen to.

"You may," Grace said, her voice even.

Julia took the pencil and wrote, in small block letters beneath the main text:

"Warm hands lead to warmer hearts."

Grace stared at it.

It wasn't polished. It wasn't clever. It was perfect.

From that moment, Julia spoke a little more each day. Only to Grace at first, then to Nathan when he dropped by with parcels, and eventually even to customers who asked questions at the counter. Her voice was soft, but steady. Unapologetic.

One evening, Grace returned from a supply run to find Julia standing behind the printing press with a fresh run of leaflets she had laid out herself. The ink was a bit smudged. The alignment crooked. But the headline glowed:

"YOU MATTER. Don't let the cold convince you otherwise."

Grace said nothing at first. She simply walked over, picked up one of the leaflets, and pressed a kiss to the top of Julia's head.

"You've found it," she whispered.

"Found what?"

"Your voice."

Julia looked down. "It's still small."

Grace smiled. "So was mine, once."

That night, Julia crawled onto the old sofa in Grace's apartment above the shop, wrapped in the quilt she'd claimed as her own. She clutched a book to her chest and stared out the window at the snow drifting between the chimneys.

"Were you scared?" she asked.

Grace, seated at her desk, looked up. "When?"

"When you were little. When no one listened."

Grace leaned back in her chair. "I still am, sometimes. But now I speak anyway."

Julia nodded. "I think… I want to be like you."

Grace crossed the room and knelt beside the sofa. "You already are."

And in that quiet, candlelit moment, something passed between them that had no need of explanation.

A trust. A bond. A shared scar healed not with time—but with tenderness.

The next morning, Tim visited the shop. Grace handed him one of Julia's new flyers without comment.

He read the message. Then he read it again.

"She wrote this?"

Grace nodded. "And printed a hundred before I got back from the supplier."

Tim tucked one gently into his coat pocket. "You should add her name to the ledger."

"I was hoping you would," Grace said. "She earned it."

That night, Tim opened the ledger and turned to a fresh page.

He wrote:

Julia – voice like snowlight.
Soft. Bright. Unmissable.

Then beneath it:

"She reminded me of Grace. And
also of the girl she used to be."

The ink dried slowly.

Some names, he thought, were less recorded than revealed.

Chapter 28

The wind had shifted.

It wasn't colder—at least not in any physical sense. But Tim felt it in his bones, in the way the days grew shorter even as spring threatened the corners of rooftops and windowpanes. He moved slower now. His hands trembled more. The ledger, once lifted with ease, now required effort.

The doctor had used words like exhaustion and overstrain, spoken in the calm tones of a man who didn't want to frighten, only to prepare.

Tim had smiled. "I've been tired for years," he said. "It's how you know you're still giving."

And yet... he knew.

He wasn't dying. Not today. Maybe not even tomorrow. But he was nearing a season of stillness. A winter of the body, even if not the calendar.

So he prepared.

He began with the letters. One to Grace. One to Peter. One to Belinda. He thanked them. Not for what they'd done for him—but for what they'd continued in his name, and in Scrooge's name before that.

He placed each one in a small envelope, sealed with wax, and tied together with twine.

Then came the ledger.

He spent a full morning reading every entry—every name, every act, every note scrawled in the margins. There were patterns. Echoes. Some entries were so faint they read like ghost stories. Others were bold and urgent.

And at the back, he found the second envelope Scrooge had left—the one marked:

"For the One Who Comes Next."

He had never opened it.

Now, he did.

Inside was a single piece of thick parchment, blank except for the top line:

"Name: _____"

"Because kindness cannot die with us."

Tim stared at the paper for a long time.

He thought of Nathan. Of Julia. Of the girl named Elsie who still visited the warming room each Thursday with her doll and her stories.

Any one of them could be next.

All of them could.

But one name rose like a star in his mind.

He took his pen, dipped it in the well, and wrote:

Julia.

Then, below it, he added:

"She reminds me that healing isn't loud. It is quiet. And relentless."

He folded the paper and placed it inside the back cover of the ledger, behind all the entries.

Then he sat back, exhaled, and looked at the fire.

It burned steadily—small but unwavering.

Like the gift itself.

Later that night, Grace found him asleep in the chair, the ledger resting on the table beside him, the fire still warm.

She covered him with a blanket.

Saw the envelope.

And understood.

CHAPTER 29

THE DAY THE LEDGER WAS passed on, the sky was the color of pewter.

Clouds hung low over London, heavy with the weight of unfallen rain, and the bells of St. Martin's rang noon with a sound that echoed off the stone like memory.

Grace walked slowly through the streets, the old leather-bound book wrapped carefully in a linen cloth, held close to her chest. She had read Tim's note twice. Once alone, and once aloud to Julia, who had said nothing for a long while afterward—just stared at the flickering hearthlight as if trying to make sense of the shadows.

Now they walked together—Grace steady, Julia silent.

The door to the Cratchit Foundation creaked open when they arrived. Nathan was inside, already setting up for the next day's distribution. He looked up, wiping his ink-stained hands on his apron, and frowned.

"Where's Tim?"

Grace said nothing, only placed the bundle on the desk.

Nathan unwrapped it slowly, revealing the ledger beneath. He ran a hand across the cover.

And then he saw the final note.

He read it once. Then again. Then met Grace's eyes.

"It's time," she said softly.

Julia stepped forward. Her hands trembled slightly as she picked up the ledger and held it as if it were made of glass.

"What do I do with it?" she whispered.

Grace smiled. "What you already do. See people. Write their names. Carry their stories. And never stop believing they matter."

Julia opened the book. The parchment inside bore her name now. Written in Tim's careful hand.

She traced the letters like they were holy.

And then she turned to a blank page.

After a moment, she wrote:

Elsie – dreams in drawings.
Wears hope like a ribbon.

Then:

> *Isaac – lost his brother. Laughed for the first time today.*

Alia – sings to her baby sister while waiting for soup.
She paused. Looked up.
Grace nodded.
Julia turned back and added a final line:

> *The gift continues.*

That evening, Grace walked alone through Camden Lane.
The lamps flickered to life one by one, painting the cobblestones in puddles of gold. Somewhere, a violin played near an open window. The scent of chestnuts drifted through the air.
She passed the Cratchit home. The curtains were drawn. The hearth inside glowed faintly.
And in the front window, a single candle burned.
Not for tradition.
Not for mourning.
But for invitation.
A light for someone cold.
Someone unseen.

Someone next.

And high above the rooftops, in the thinning clouds, the first stars began to appear.

Lesser-Known Facts About Charles Dickens' A Christmas Carol

Many readers don't realize that Charles Dickens wrote A Christmas Carol in just six weeks. Driven by financial strain and the weight of personal debt, he composed the story under immense pressure—but what emerged became a timeless holiday treasure.

Remarkably, Dickens chose to self-publish the novella. He printed 6,000 copies, which sold out by Christmas Eve. Though the book was a commercial hit with the public, Dickens didn't reap much profit. He had covered the printing costs himself, and his vision for an elegant physical edition—complete with gilt-edged pages and illustrations—cut deeply into his earnings.

Dickens also had a gift for performance. He often read the story aloud in packed halls, and his dramatic flair brought Scrooge, Marley, and the spirits vividly to life. These readings became so popular that Dickens toured widely with them, reinforcing the story's cultural impact.

One fascinating legacy of the book is its role in popularizing the phrase "Merry Christmas." While the greeting existed before, Dickens' story helped embed it in the modern vernacular.

And despite its iconic ring, "Bah, humbug!" is only said twice by Scrooge in the original text. Still, the phrase quickly became synonymous with holiday grumpiness.

Over the years, A Christmas Carol has been adapted for the screen more than twenty times, in forms ranging from silent films to musicals and animated specials.

Interestingly, Dickens often developed his stories while walking. He would take long, solitary strolls through the streets of London at night, mulling over character arcs and dialogue in his mind—A Christmas Carol included.

And in early drafts, Jacob Marley wasn't even a ghost. He was originally portrayed as still alive, a business partner haunting Scrooge in a more figurative sense. Dickens eventually revised the character into the specter we now recognize, creating one of literature's most enduring supernatural figures.

These small details and lesser-known facts only deepen the appreciation for what Dickens accomplished. A Christmas Carol remains a tale that grows richer with every telling, inspiring not only generations of readers—but also this very story.

England at the Time of A Christmas Carol

The early 19th century was a time of upheaval and transformation in England. The Industrial Revolution was in full swing, reshaping the nation's economy and social structure. Cities like London grew rapidly as people flocked from rural areas to find work in factories and mills. But with progress came hardship. Overcrowding, pollution, and inadequate housing defined much of urban life. Poverty was rampant. Living conditions for the working class were often squalid and dangerous.

Social divisions were stark. While the upper classes enjoyed privilege and prosperity, the poor struggled to survive. Child labor was widespread. Access to healthcare and education was minimal for those without means. It was a society straining under the weight of inequality—and it was this reality that Charles Dickens knew all too well.

Charles Dickens was more than a storyteller. He was a social reformer who wielded his pen to expose the injustices of his time. His own childhood was marked by poverty, and those early struggles left a deep and lasting impression. His novels did more than entertain—they challenged society to confront the inhumanity that industrial progress too often ignored.

A Christmas Carol is a direct product of that mission. Through its vivid characters and moral clarity, Dickens offered not just a ghost story—but a wake-up call.

The spectral visitors who confront Ebenezer Scrooge are more than supernatural plot devices. They serve as powerful metaphors for accountability, memory, and the potential for change.

Jacob Marley, bound in chains forged by greed and selfishness, represents the consequences of a life spent ignoring others. His warning to Scrooge is also a warning to Victorian society: reform or be damned to regret.

The Ghosts of Christmas Past, Present, and Yet to Come reveal not only Scrooge's personal failings, but the suffering of families like the Cratchits—ordinary people overlooked by the powerful. Through them, Dickens holds up a mirror to the world and demands we see what our indifference has wrought.

Dickens chose Christmas for a reason. In the bleakness of industrial London, the holiday stood as a rare moment of unity and generosity. It was a time when even the coldest hearts could thaw.

Scrooge's transformation—from miser to benefactor—demonstrates Dickens' belief in personal redemption and societal healing. The story insists that change is not only possible, but essential. And it begins with a choice: to see others, to care, and to act.

Though A Christmas Carol was written in response to Victorian-era struggles, its message is timeless. In a world still marked by inequality and disconnection, Dickens' call for compassion and social responsibility continues to resonate.

His story reminds us that no act of kindness is too small. That we are all connected. That redemption is always possible—for people and for society.

As we revisit A Christmas Carol each holiday season, we're not just enjoying a literary classic—we're accepting an invitation. To reflect. To give. To believe in the better angels of our nature.

Also available from the author for the holidays:

A Christmas Carol

Ebenezer Scrooge thought his transformation was complete after the spirits departed that fateful Christmas Eve—but his true journey was only beginning. In this heartwarming and adventurous continuation of Charles Dickens' classic tale, Scrooge awakens on Christmas morning determined to live by the spirit of goodwill, generosity, and love every day.

As Scrooge tries to put his past behind him, he faces new challenges that test his resolve, from the lingering ghosts of his past mistakes to the difficulties of helping those in need. With the support of his nephew Fred, the Cratchit family, and the community he once alienated, Scrooge embarks on a journey of redemption that proves change is not just a single moment but an ongoing commitment.

Filled with laughter, heartfelt moments, and a deep exploration of the impact one man's transformation can have on those around him, A Christmas Carol: The Next Chapter is a story of hope, renewal, and the enduring power of the Christmas spirit.

The Hidden Workshop

The Hidden Workshop delves into the intricate dynamics of family, legacy, and redemption against the backdrop of a snow-covered log cabin nestled deep in the woods. Uncle Frank, a master wood carver of unparalleled skill, has spent years honing his craft in the solitude of his workshop, adjacent to the cozy cabin where he once shared a life with his beloved wife. After her passing, Uncle Frank withdrew from the world, immersing himself in his carvings and selling his intricate toys to toy stores far and wide.

As Uncle Frank's health deteriorates due to terminal cancer, he shocks his family by extending an invitation for a Christmas reunion at the cabin, a tradition he had abandoned after his wife's death. The family's excitement is tinged with surprise and apprehension as they gather under the snowy boughs of the forest.

A Christmas Carousel

Samantha Bennett, a career-driven journalist in her early 30s, finds herself in a familiar yet distant place—her childhood hometown of Mapletown. Assigned by her editor to cover the restoration of an old Christmas carousel for the town's Christmas Festival, Samantha reluctantly leaves the bustling streets of New York City for the nostalgic charm of the small town she hasn't visited in over a decade. Haunted by memories of her late mother and a difficult departure from the place she once called home, Samantha sees the assignment as both a challenge and an opportunity for closure.

Upon her arrival, Samantha is greeted by the warmth of Mapletown and its people, especially Mrs. Keegan, the owner of the local inn, who welcomes her back with open arms. The town is blanketed in snow, dressed in festive decorations, and bustling with excitement as Christmas approaches. At the heart of the excitement lies the beloved carousel, a historic piece that holds cherished memories for generations of Mapletown residents, including Samantha herself. But a developer has different plans.

www.ingramcontent.com/pod-product-compliance
Lightning Source LLC
LaVergne TN
LVHW041337080426
835512LV00006B/498